Bellingham
Public Library

OCT   2018

Bellingham, Ma 02019
508-966-1660

S0-CFO-281

Careers in Food and Agriculture

Stuart A. Kallen

ReferencePoint Press®

© 2018 ReferencePoint Press, Inc.
Printed in the United States

For more information, contact:
ReferencePoint Press, Inc.
PO Box 27779
San Diego, CA 92198
www.ReferencePointPress.com

ALL RIGHTS RESERVED.
No part of this work covered by the copyright hereon may be reproduced or used in any form or by any means—graphic, electronic, or mechanical, including photocopying, recording, taping, web distribution, or information storage retrieval systems—without the written permission of the publisher.

Picture credits:
 6: Maury Aaseng
 9: Shutterstock/Syda Productions
49: Shutterstock.com/Blend Images
57: Shutterstock/Joshua Rainey Photography

LIBRARY OF CONGRESS CATALOGING-IN-PUBLICATION DATA

Name: Kallen, Stuart A., 1955– author.
Title: Careers in Food and Agriculture/by Stuart A. Kallen.
Description: San Diego, CA: ReferencePoint Press, Inc., 2017. | Series: Exploring Careers | Includes bibliographical references and index.
Identifiers: LCCN 2017040657 (print) | LCCN 2017045825 (ebook) | ISBN 9781682823125 (eBook) | ISBN 9781682823118 (hardback)
Subjects: LCSH: Agriculture—Vocational guidance—Juvenile literature. | Food—Vocational guidance—Juvenile literature.
Classification: LCC S494.5.A4 (ebook) | LCC S494.5.A4 K35 2017 (print) | DDC 338.1023—dc23
LC record available at https://lccn.loc.gov/2017040657

Contents

Seeing the World Through Food

All people must eat, and in the United States more than 21 million people work every day in the food and agricultural industries. These workers plant and harvest crops, design food processing equipment, oversee food and beverage production facilities, and use science and technology to devise new ways to feed the hungry masses. Numerous jobs are focused on food advertising, distribution, product research, and health and safety regulations. Food and agricultural professionals like chef Bobby Flay spend a lot of time thinking about food. "I wake up every morning and see the word 'FOOD' written in the sky; I see the whole world through food," Flay told *National Geographic* in 2014.

There are many familiar jobs in the food and agricultural industries, such as farmer, chef, butcher, food safety inspector, nutritionist, and restaurant manager. However, some jobs in food and agriculture are unknown to the general public. Food microbiologists monitor the effects of bacteria, viruses, algae, fungi, and other microorganisms on plants, animals, and food products. Food lawyers specialize in food-system laws concerning labor contracts, environmental regulations, international trade, patents, and labeling rules. Food stylists arrange food to look incredibly appealing in photos that appear in menus, cookbooks, magazines, and ads.

With the wide variety of jobs, it is no wonder the food and agricultural industries contributed nearly a trillion dollars to the US economy in 2015, according to the US Department of Agriculture

(USDA). And that economic impact is expected to grow. A 2016 forecast by the industry group Food Packaging Trends and Advances says the food production industry will expand at a steady 3 percent annual rate through 2022. Farmers and ranchers can also expect to see a rising demand for their products throughout the world. A 2016 study by the United Nations predicts that global food demand is expected to increase by 80 percent by 2050.

Where the Jobs Are

Most people associate food production with farming and ranching, but that sector only makes up 15 percent of the food production business. About 42 percent of the available jobs in food and agriculture are in business and management. Major food processors like Tyson Foods, Kraft Heinz, and Campbell's Soup Company need production-facility managers, financial administrators, and marketing directors. The food and agricultural industries are also increasingly embracing globalization, and experts predict there will be a growing need for college-educated workers with foreign-language skills who are interested in international finance and global food policy.

About one-third of the jobs in food and agriculture are in the STEM fields (science, technology, engineering, and math). Food producers need scientists who specialize in genetics, reproduction, growth, and diseases in plants and animals. As food producers strive to stay on top of the latest digital trends, workers with technology degrees are in high demand in nearly every niche of the industries. Agricultural machinery producers are looking for engineers to design and test farm machinery, processing tools, and other equipment.

As the demand grows for highly educated workers, the USDA predicts that the food and agricultural industries will produce 57,900 jobs for college graduates every year through 2020. However, agricultural colleges such as Iowa State University and the University of Kentucky College of Agriculture are only producing 35,400 graduates per year. This shortfall means 22,500 jobs will go unfilled or will be filled by nonagricultural majors. But those with agricultural degrees are preferred because these graduates understand the various environments and technical terminology of the industries.

Careers in Food and Agriculture

Occupation	Minimum Educational Requirement	2016 Median Pay
Agricultural engineer	Bachelor's degree	$73,640
Agricultural and food scientist	Bachelor's degree	$62,920
Baker	No formal educational requirements	$25,090
Biological technician	Bachelor's degree	$42,520
Butcher	No formal educational requirements	$29,870
Farmer, rancher, and other agricultural manager	High school diploma or equivalent	$66,360
Food service manager	High school diploma or equivalent	$50,820
Heavy vehicle and mobile equipment service technician	High school diploma or equivalent	$47,690
Microbiologist	Bachelor's degree	$66,850
Dietitian and nutritionist	Bachelor's degree	$58,920

Source: Bureau of Labor Statistics, *Occupational Outlook Handbook*, 2015. www.bls.gov.

Good Pay, Low Tuition

Many food and agricultural jobs offer decent salaries and benefits, according to PayScale, an online information company specializing in salaries, benefits, and compensation. Whereas the median salary for all US jobs in 2017 was $45,000, food and agriculture jobs provided a median salary of $47,300, with $5,000 in yearly bonuses. Managers of food processing plants averaged nearly $61,000, and information technology managers at food and agricultural businesses brought in an average of $78,500.

Although food and agricultural salaries tend to be above average, the cost of obtaining a degree in the field is often lower than the cost of other degrees. The majority of agricultural colleges are part of state land-grant universities. Land-grant universities were established during the nineteenth century to focus on education in agriculture, science, and engineering (as opposed to education in liberal arts). Tuition at land-grant universities is much lower than at private colleges. Savings are even better for students who attend land-grant colleges in their home states and pay in-state tuition rates.

Students who pursue careers in food and agriculture will find themselves at a financial advantage. They can graduate college with less student debt, provide skills that are in great demand, and earn more money than average workers. And as agricultural blogger Amanda Radke writes in a 2015 article in *Beef* magazine, "While agriculture is a multi-billion dollar industry that directly affects everyone in the world each day, employers still struggle to find qualified candidates that are enthusiastic about the industry."

As long as people keep eating, there will always be jobs in producing, processing, distributing, and selling food. Anyone looking for rewarding and secure employment can take a trip to the grocery store or gaze out over fields of crops and see their future in the food and agricultural industries that provide the most necessary commodities on Earth.

Farmer

What Does a Farmer Do?

Farming is one of the oldest occupations in human history, and for centuries there was little change in the way crops were grown, livestock was raised, and dairy products were produced. But farming is evolving rapidly during the twenty-first century. A new generation of farmers is employing drones, digital sensors, cloud computing, and other so-called smart-farming techniques to improve yields, reduce chemical use, and decrease water consumption. Some family farmers are turning away from traditional crops like corn and soybeans to produce more profitable, value-added commodities like bamboo, fish, organic vegetables, and gourmet cheeses.

The face of farming is also changing. According to the most recent data by the Economic Research Service of the USDA, the number of female-operated farms more than doubled between 1982 and 2012. In 2014 women made up 30 percent of America's farmers and were the fastest-growing demographic in small-scale and organic operations. As Kathleen Merrigan, a former USDA deputy

At a Glance

Farmer

Minimum Educational Requirements

High school diploma

Personal Qualities

Hard worker, mechanically inclined, good math and business skills, able to handle large machinery

Certification and Licensing

Voluntary

Working Conditions

Long hours outdoors, often in extreme weather conditions, in barns, animal stalls, and fields

Salary

$66,360 annually in 2016

Number of Jobs

929,800 in 2014

Future Job Outlook

Decline in some areas; growth in others

secretary, recently told the independent news outlet *Grist*, "Women want to be outside, they want to be near family. There's lots of interest in where our food comes from, how it is grown. We are seeing more [female] beginning farmers coming in and I think the trend is going to continue."

Whatever the farmer's gender or background, those who work in what is sometimes called direct agriculture satisfy the dietary needs of over 324 million Americans every day. American farmers also feed the world; one-third of all farm goods are exported to other countries. And farming remains a big business; the output of America's 929,800 farmers contributed almost $137 billion to the economy in 2015.

A large majority of agricultural producers own small farms. In 2016 only 4 percent of American farms were considered large, meaning they were over 2,000 acres (809 ha); 96 percent were classified as small farms, farming around 250 acres (101 ha). Nine out of

A farmer distributes food to his cows. Some farmers grow crops; others raise livestock. Some do both. Whatever their focus, farming requires hard work, long hours, and a great deal of technical and product knowledge.

ten of the small farms were family owned. Family farmers perform almost all chores necessary to keep their operation running, including planting seeds, fertilizing plants, eliminating weeds and insects, harvesting crops, and handling livestock. To be successful, farmers must be knowledgeable about soil conditions and plant and animal diseases. Farmers need strong mechanical skills to operate, maintain, and repair large machines like combines, cultivators, tractors, trucks, and conveyors. Farmers also deal with smaller equipment, such as milking machines, grain grinders, and chain saws. Additionally, farmers need to repair and maintain farm infrastructure, such as irrigation systems, sewers, buildings, fences, and animal shelters.

Farming is a tough and unpredictable business dictated by weather and crop prices forecast several months in the future. This means farmers must have a strong understanding of agricultural business and economics. Farmers often borrow large sums of money from banks and government agencies to purchase fuel, seeds, agricultural chemicals, livestock, and complex machinery. They act as their own sales agents to sell their commodities. Prices of crops, dairy products, and livestock fluctuate daily. Oftentimes this means planting a mix of crops to ensure a profit in case the price of one or more crops declines. Farmers must also navigate complex programs, such as crop insurance and federal farm subsidies, which can provide a monetary cushion when prices fall. And like any small business owner, farmers are required to keep financial and tax records and follow state and federal employment regulations when hiring and firing workers.

As farming becomes more sophisticated and reliant on technology, farmers will need a thorough knowledge of agricultural software, as twenty-four-year-old farmer Mike Milligan of Cass City, Michigan, explains on the agricultural news website AgWeb:

> [I use] precision ag software to improve fertilizer efficiencies, crop yields and sustainability. Today's software allows producers to maximize every acre in their fields. I have used the software to create management zones with every field we farm. I use it to adjust rates of fertilizer and seed to each zone. I hope to incorporate different chemical rates into the zones in the future.

How Do You Become a Farmer?

Education

Most farmers learn to farm from their parents, grandparents, and even great-grandparents, and many get by with only a high school education. However, the agricultural business is competitive, and many farmers who have been following traditional practices are finding it difficult to earn a living. Students who earn a bachelor's degree in agriculture will have a business edge. Curricula vary among institutions, but most land-grant universities offer courses in agricultural economics, agricultural markets and prices, the economics of natural resources, farming and natural resources, farm and ranch management, plant and animal breeding, and dairy science.

Young women interested in direct agriculture can also participate in Annie's Project, a national program designed to empower female farmers. Classes cover farm and ranch business, management, and operations, and they are offered through local farm extension offices. Since 2003, Annie's Project has provided an education to more than eight thousand women in thirty states. As Reid Young of the University of Illinois Extension explains on the school's website, "Women are taught the basics of managing money, how property is titled, setting up farm leases, basic grain marketing, deciding on insurance products, and putting together a business plan which includes financial documents like balance sheets, income statements and cash flows."

Certification

College graduates with a four-year degree in agriculture who complete an eighty-five-hour land management program can obtain accreditation from the American Society of Farm Managers and Rural Appraisers (ASFMRA), which offers the accredited farm manager certificate. The accreditation proves the holder is knowledgeable in crop and livestock production, commodity marketing, soil conservation, financial analysis and accounting, and farm real estate brokerage. The ASFMRA also offers certification as an accredited agricultural consultant for those who wish to advise farmers on financial and business matters, human resources and personnel management, and production and operation.

Apprenticeships

In 2016 only 6 percent of farmers were under the age of thirty-five, and about 25 percent were over sixty-five. That means young farmers are in high demand. High school students interested in meeting that demand can begin their education by joining the student organization Future Farmers of America (FFA), which provides agricultural instruction to its members. FFA members who want to learn more can work as apprentices for a season to determine whether farm life is for them. Apprentices learn to plant, harvest, weed, collect eggs, and feed animals; in exchange, they receive room and board and a small stipend.

Apprentice farmers who wish to combine organic agriculture with world travel can join Worldwide Opportunities on Organic Farms (WWOOF). Members, called WWOOFers, fill apprenticeships at more than twenty-one hundred organic farms in the United States, Africa, the Americas, the Asia-Pacific region, and Europe. WWOOFers work four to six hours a day on sustainable farms in exchange for room and board. Assignments last from one day to three or more months.

Skills and Personality

A farmer needs to be physically fit, mechanically inclined, and possess a good head for business. Farm work often involves tossing around 100-pound (45 kg) bales of hay, lifting 50-pound (23 kg) sacks of feed, and moving heavy containers of agricultural chemicals. Additionally, farmers spend their days bending, kneeling, crawling, and climbing when working around huge machines. Farmers need good mechanical skills to operate, maintain, and repair equipment. Analytical and critical-thinking skills are necessary to make decisions, determine how to improve their operations, monitor commodity prices, operate computers, and respond to the demands of changing markets.

On the Job

Employers

Most farmers are self-employed and work land that has been in their family for generations. Those who do not own land sometimes gain experience as farm managers before committing to buying or leasing farmland. Both options have positive and negative aspects. Leasing land is the cheapest way to get into farming, but prospective farmers still need to borrow money to purchase tools, seeds, animals, and other necessities. Buying is difficult for prospective farmers because agricultural land is so expensive. In 2016 the average price of an acre of Iowa farmland was $6,732, and in Illinois it was over $11,000 an acre. A farmer needs to plant at least 250 acres (101 ha) to earn a profit, which means it would take an outlay of $1.68 million in Iowa to purchase land, and the cost in Illinois would be $2.7 million.

Newcomers to the farming profession can avoid huge outlays and gain experience by pursuing alternatives to traditional farming. For example, some farmers participate in what is called community supported agriculture (CSA). The farmers use social media to sign up a network of consumers pledged to financially support their farm operation. The community shareholders put up money to cover a farmer's costs for leasing land and equipment. In return, the farmer delivers fresh—usually organic—meat, eggs, milk products, and fruits and veggies to the shareholders. By providing working capital, shareholders receive high-quality food for lower prices than they would pay at the grocery store.

Aquaculture, or fish farming, is another farming niche that tends to be less expensive than purchasing land. Fish farmers raise seafood such as tilapia, salmon, shrimp, and trout in tanks, ponds, or other enclosures. Globally, fish farming is a multibillion-dollar business that produces around half of all the seafood that is consumed. In the Midwest, fish farmers are converting unused barns, warehouses, and even old schoolhouses into farms filled with tanks full of fish. The fish farmers sell their products to grocery stores, restaurants, and walk-in customers.

Working Conditions

Farmers work outdoors in all types of weather, from sunrise to sundown seven days a week during the growing season. Those who have dairy cows and other livestock must feed and care for their animals every day. Farmers work with hazardous chemicals and machinery such as tractors and combines that can cause serious injuries.

Earnings

According to the Bureau of Labor Statistics (BLS), the median wage for farmers in 2016 was $66,360. The lowest 10 percent of farmers earned less than $35,020, and farmers in the top 10 percent earned more than $126,070. This wage gap is due to the fact that farm income can vary from year to year due to weather conditions, fluctuations in commodity prices, and other factors.

Opportunities for Advancement

Most farmers gain experience working with older farmers, usually parents and grandparents. Those who start out small in markets like organic farming or aquaculture can use their profits to expand their operations by leasing or buying more land. Some farmers move into more profitable industries, such as food processing or agricultural consulting.

What Is the Future Outlook for Farmers?

The future outlook for farmers varies by segment. The BLS predicts that the number of farmers will decline by 2 percent through 2024 as prices increase on seeds, chemicals, land, and machinery. The largest growth in farm employment will be in niche segments, such as CSA, organic farming, aquaculture, and other enterprises increasingly popular among consumers. There is little doubt that the world needs young farmers with innovative ideas. As Corey Reid, the chief executive officer of the farm equipment company John Deere, states on the USDA website, "We're looking for the best of every discipline to come into agriculture and the work going on in science, technology, engineering, and math . . . is exploding the opportunities for young people going forward. . . . There's phenomenal opportunity in our industry."

National FFA Organization
PO Box 68960
6060 FFA Dr.
Indianapolis, IN 46268-0960
website: www.ffa.org

The Future Farmers of America (FFA) is the premier student organization for those interested in agriculture and related fields. The website provides information about the history of FFA and its mission along with publications focused on agricultural education.

National Young Farmers Coalition (NYFC)
358 Warren St.
Hudson, NY 12534
website: www.youngfarmers.org

The NYFC is dedicated to helping young farmers in the United States. The website features blogs and press, plus media that provides numerous resources related to farm training, jobs, resources, land leasing, and credit.

Women's Agricultural Network (WAgN)
327 US Route 302
Berlin, VT 05641
website: www.uvm.edu/wagn

Affiliated with the University of Vermont Extension and the USDA, this organization seeks to increase the number of female farmers through education, technical assistance, and networking opportunities. The website provides books and manuals, articles, fact sheets, and materials to encourage and inform female farmers.

Worldwide Opportunities on Organic Farms USA (WWOOF-USA)
654 Fillmore St.
San Francisco, CA 94117
website: https://wwoofusa.org

Program members can sign up to spend time on organic host farms, receiving room and board while learning about sustainable agriculture. Members under age eighteen must be accompanied by a parent or guardian. Children and pets are welcome for those over eighteen.

Agricultural Scientist

What Does an Agricultural Scientist Do?

Consumers in the United States spend less money on groceries than people in any other country in the world. According to the USDA, Americans spent just 6.4 percent of their household income on food in 2016. Food in Canada cost consumers 9 percent of their income, and people in the Philippines paid a staggering 42 percent. Although most Americans do not think about such things when they go shopping, anyone who has enjoyed relatively inexpensive products like cereal, bread, chips, pasta, apples, tomatoes, and soda should thank an agricultural scientist. These professionals, sometimes referred to as agronomists, devote their lives to the science and technology of producing plants cheaply and efficiently for food, fiber, and fuel.

Agricultural scientists focus on maintaining a safe and reliable food supply in the United States and in countries throughout the world. They are experts in irrigation, fertilization, weed control,

At a Glance

Agricultural Scientist

Minimum Educational Requirements
Bachelor's degree

Personal Qualities
Analytical, critical thinker, detail oriented, good communicator, business and math skills

Certification and Licensing
Voluntary

Working Conditions
Indoors in offices and laboratories; outdoors in all types of weather in agricultural settings

Salary
$62,920 annually in 2016

Number of Jobs
36,100 in 2014

Future Job Outlook
5 percent growth through 2024

seed varieties, and other aspects of growing crops. For instance, they need to demonstrate knowledge of plant pests and plant diseases.

Agricultural scientists might specialize in a number of disciplines, including plant genetics, soil science, plant physiology, biology, chemistry, ecology, earth science, and meteorology (weather). Some concentrate on developing drought-resistant crops and conduct research and development focused on improving irrigation techniques. Those who focus on the economics of agricultural resource production use math and analytics to study complex questions about how best to use environmental, natural, and human resources to produce food.

Soil scientists specialize in conserving soil, preventing erosion, and controlling pollution from farm chemicals. They study the physical and chemical properties of the soil and advise farmers about soil-related problems. Soil scientists develop plans to increase soil nutrients and design integrated pest management (IPM) strategies to eliminate weeds and harmful insects without the use of chemicals. Some soil scientists focus on sustainable agriculture, which involves three primary objectives: a healthy environment, economic profitability, and social and economic equity. American soil scientist Ray Archuleta believes sustainable agriculture can be integrated with modern industrial growing practices to protect the environment. "We should have been mimicking nature all along instead of trying to control it with [herbicides], fungicides, and insecticides," Archuleta says in an interview with the Agriculture.com website. "We should have been nurturing and facilitating the soil. We needed to be wise and cautious with our tools."

Whatever their specialty, agricultural scientists spend their days collecting, analyzing, and interpreting scientific data. They physically inspect farm fields, walking between rows of crops to study soil and plants. Agricultural scientists also use photos of fields taken by aircraft or satellites. Those who work with cutting-edge technology use low-flying drones with high-definition cameras. The drones take thousands of photos that are assembled into extremely accurate two-dimensional or three-dimensional maps to show exactly where there are problems in the field. With the highly specific data, agricultural scientists can practice what is called precision agriculture, which tailors the use of fertilizer, water, and chemicals in specific locations in a field.

How Do You Become an Agricultural Scientist?

Education

Agricultural scientists are the ultimate STEM scholars, and high school students with an eye on the profession should focus on advanced courses in science, technology, engineering, and math. After high school, students should set their sights on attending a land-grant college while pursuing a bachelor's degree in agricultural science, agricultural biochemistry, or related biology or chemistry fields. Undergraduate course work includes biology, chemistry, botany, and plant conservation. Courses are conducted in classrooms and labs. Those who wish to become soil scientists should focus on plant pathology, soil chemistry, biochemistry, and entomology (the study of insects). Although a focus on STEM topics is necessary, prospective agricultural scientists can sharpen their job skills by taking courses in communications, finance, computer science, and sociology.

Many good jobs are available for those with bachelor's degrees in agricultural science, but the best positions and highest salaries are available to those who obtain a master's degree or a doctorate. Advanced degrees in agricultural science, plant physiology, or soil science are necessary for those who wish to teach college, conduct research, or pursue other advanced positions. Undergraduates who wish to obtain advanced degrees first need to study for and pass the graduate school entrance exam.

Certification and Licensing

Certification is not necessary for most agricultural scientists, but accreditation is a standard by which professionals are judged and can be useful for advancing a career. The American Society of Agronomy offers several certifications. Agricultural scientists who work in IPM can obtain a resistance management specialty certification, and those who specialize in sustainable crops and management can acquire a sustainability specialty certification. Consultants who spend their time advising growers and farm managers can obtain a certified crop adviser or certified professional agronomist accreditation. These certifications are widely recognized by agriculture-related industries, academia, and government. Applicants with a bachelor of science degree in agronomy are required to have at least two years of work experience. Those with an associate's degree in an agronomy-related field need three years of experience for certification. Applicants without a college degree are required to show four years of work experience. Certification requires applicants to pass two comprehensive exams.

Nine states require soil scientists to be licensed: Maine, Minnesota, Virginia, Wisconsin, Texas, Tennessee, South Carolina, North Carolina, and North Dakota. Most automatically grant licenses to those with bachelor's degrees in soil science or holders of a certified professional soil scientist accreditation from the Soil Science Society of America. Qualification for certification is generally based on education, previous professional experience, and successfully completing a comprehensive exam.

Getting Experience and Internships

High school students can get an introduction to basic agricultural science by joining the 4-H youth organization or Future Farmers of America (FFA). 4-H consists of ninety thousand local clubs and is affiliated with organizations in over fifty countries. In the United States, 4-H has more than 6.5 million members between the ages of five and twenty-one. Agriculture was the original focus of 4-H, but the organization now offers science, engineering, and technology programs. FFA promotes agricultural education and careers. The organization hosts career development events in which members compete in contests to test their skills in food science, agronomy, business, mechanics, marketing and sales, and numerous other topics.

High school and college students can participate in internship programs. Those who work as interns on farms get hands-on experience working with crops, breeding animals, and practicing sustainable growing techniques. Michael Swoish, who has a doctorate in soil science, told the website AgDaily, an agricultural news source, about the importance of farm internships: "Internships or working on a farm prior to/during your ag degree can be invaluable in terms of gaining experience and figuring out what's important to know. Learning the jargon of the industry and which issues trouble farmers the most are two other very important skills that you won't necessarily pick up in the classroom."

Prospective agricultural scientists who wish to work in a more corporate environment can gain experience at large agribusiness companies. Monsanto and Bayer provide summer internship opportunities to students enrolled in full-time degree programs at the bachelor, master, and doctoral levels. These companies search for candidates who are majoring in agribusiness, agronomy, biochemistry, molecular biology, chemistry, agricultural business administration, and mechanical engineering.

Skills and Personality

Agricultural scientists usually have a strong interest in agriculture, the environment, and natural resources. The work involves researching problems and formulating workable solutions. This requires agricultural scientists to use skills like critical thinking, data analysis, and math to analyze vast amounts of data. A good background in computer science is also required for those who design custom software for conducting research.

Agricultural scientists often work closely with those who do not have professional knowledge. They need good communication skills and patience to explain complex solutions to farmers, food processors, and other clients. Business skills and a good understanding of agricultural economics are also important for those who consult with growers about purchasing new equipment and instituting new systems for food production.

On the Job

Employers

Agricultural scientists work for a variety of institutions, including colleges and universities; food manufacturers; agribusiness companies; biotechnology firms; environmental research organizations; agricultural consulting services; and local, state, and federal governments. Agricultural scientists are employed by facilities that produce cotton, wool, and other types of cloth made from natural fibers. Some work in the ethanol production industry, creating motor fuel from corn and other plants. Those with advanced degrees are conducting research for companies working to produce the next generation of biofuels from plants and other natural products.

Working Conditions

Agricultural scientists spend about half their time conducting field-work at farms, nurseries, greenhouses, and other food-growing sites; the other half is spent in laboratories and offices. They generally work forty hours per week, with most office and lab work being conducted during business hours. However, visits to farms often take place in the early morning hours, and there is occasional weekend work. Fieldwork requires agricultural scientists to be outside in all weather conditions, including rain, snow, and extreme temperatures. Those who visit food production sites must wear suitable clothing, such as goggles, disposable footwear, and hard hats. These facilities are often noisy, cold, and filled with dangerous machinery.

Earnings

According to the Bureau of Labor Statistics (BLS) the median annual wage in 2016 for agricultural scientists was $62,920. The median wage represents the salary at which half the workers earned more and half earned less. The lowest-paid 10 percent of agricultural scientists earned less than $37,660, and the highest-paid 10 percent earned more than $116,520. Most employers offer agricultural scientists standard benefits packages that include medical benefits, paid vacations, and other perks.

Opportunities for Advancement

Employers of agricultural scientists, including government agencies and large corporations, offer regular promotions and salary increases. Beginning agricultural scientists might start off in basic research, working in labs with many others. As they gain experience, agricultural scientists might get assigned to their own labs while taking on supervisory roles. Those with experience will have greater access to research grants and might have opportunities for travel to conferences and conventions.

What Is the Future Outlook for Agricultural Scientists?

The BLS forecasts that the market for agricultural scientists will grow 5 percent through 2024. Growth will be fueled by continuing research into agricultural production methods and an increasing demand for food due to population growth. Certain specializations, such as those related to sustainability, biotechnology, and food supply and safety are predicted to grow at a steady rate. Additionally, the job is quite stable—as long as people must eat, agricultural scientists will be in demand despite the state of the general economy.

Find Out More

American Society of Agronomy (ASA)
5585 Guilford Rd.
Fitchburg, WI 53711
website: www.agronomy.org

The ASA exists to empower agricultural scientists, educators, and practitioners to develop and apply sustainable agronomic solutions to feed the world. The group offers certification, career information, and educational programs that feature live webinars and online learning videos.

Appropriate Technology Transfer to Rural Areas (ATTRA)
PO Box 3838
Butte, MT 59702
website: https://attra.ncat.org

ATTRA is committed to providing information and technical assistance to those involved in sustainable agriculture in the United States, including farmers, ranchers, extension agents, educators, and others. ATTRA's website contains educational information, webinars, and information about internships.

National Institute of Food and Agriculture (NIFA)
800 Ninth St. SW
Washington, DC 20024
website: https://nifa.usda.gov

NIFA is the division of the USDA that provides funding for programs that advance the understanding of agricultural science. NIFA oversees the 4-H organization and offers educational programs, research grants, and comprehensive information about farming, ranching, plants, food, and the environment.

Soil Science Society of America (SSSA)
5585 Guilford Rd.
Fitchburg, WI 53711
website: www.soils.org

The SSSA is a scientific society dedicated to research and education concerning sustainable soils worldwide. The society's website features a wide array of content for students, from kindergarteners to college graduates. The SSSA also offers career advice, scholarships, and certification programs.

Food Production Manager

At a Glance

Food Production Manager

Minimum Educational Requirements

None; bachelor's of science degree preferred

Personal Qualities

Communication skills, problem-solving abilities, tech skills, mechanically inclined

Certification and Licensing

Certifications required by some employers

Working Conditions

Full-time work in offices and on production floors where hard hats, safety glasses, and other gear is required for protection

Salary

$97,140 median annual salary in 2016

Number of Jobs

90,630 in 2016

Future Job Outlook

Some decline for all industrial production managers, but ample opportunities remain for food production managers

What Does a Food Production Manager Do?

In 2016 scientist Carlos Monteiro studied American diets. He discovered that 60 percent of the average American's calories come from processed foods. The study defined processed foods as those with flavors, colors, sweeteners, oils, and other additives that people do not usually cook with at home. These products include soft drinks, salty snacks, cakes, pizza, canned goods, and frozen meals. These foods—and many others—are produced at facilities overseen by food production managers. These professionals supervise workers as they turn vegetables, grains, beans, sugar, dairy, meats, seafood, and other raw foodstuffs into the products that line the shelves of supermarkets, convenience marts, and other stores that sell food.

Food production managers are often referred to as plant managers. They create production schedules, oversee plant operations, and perform management duties. They ensure quotas are met, tend to budgetary matters, and work to reduce costs, maintain quality, and ensure that their facility complies with all federal, state, and local regulations.

Food production managers hire, train, and fire workers and strive to maintain a harmonious work environment by discussing issues and solving staff problems when they arise. They guarantee smooth plant operations by working with maintenance staff to ensure that production equipment and other machinery is properly maintained, repaired, and replaced when necessary. Plant managers also work with people who are not on the production floor, including corporate office personnel, human resources, contractors, suppliers, buyers, and sales and marketing personnel.

Food production managers supervise numerous processes that require them to have firsthand knowledge of industrial food production techniques. This might involve the cleaning and sorting of fruits and vegetables, the slaughter and smoking of meat, or ingredients used in packaged food. Waste management is also part of the job. Food production managers monitor processes to determine the amount of food scraps produced and work to reduce waste. They also ensure that waste is properly handled to comply with industry standards and environmental laws.

During the numerous production processes, quality control is of the utmost importance for a food production manager. Contaminated food can force a plant closure and cause widespread illness and even death. This requires food production managers to take a proactive role in maintaining a culture of safety. They oversee safety committees that identify hazards, schedule safety training sessions, issue safety committee reports, and implement improvements to provide a safer working environment. When accidents occur, food production managers write reports and take steps to prevent further problems.

Food production managers have numerous bureaucratic tasks. They write monthly reports on topics such as quality control, plant efficiency, environmental compliance, and employee performance.

They work on budgets with accountants and corporate executives and prepare presentations with research and development teams. This work requires food production managers to maintain a high level of discretion; production goals and information about personnel and plant operations needs to be kept confidential.

How Do You Become a Food Production Manager?

Education

There are no education standards for food production managers, but employers prefer those who hold at least a bachelor of science degree. Acceptable majors include food science, food technology, microbiology, food engineering, or production and operations management. Students in food science classes learn about food chemistry, regulations, food safety and quality control, and food preservation. Microbiology students focus on the behavior of bacteria, viruses, algae, and fungi, and they learn about the way microorganisms contaminate plants, animals, and other food products. Those who major in food engineering study physics, chemistry, mathematics, food machinery and instrumentation, packaging technology, and waste treatment systems. Operations management courses cover the technology, mechanics, and production methods used in food factories. Students can also benefit by taking courses in business administration and consumer economics.

Some food production managers hold graduate degrees, such as a master of science in food science and technology. Graduate students learn about chemistry, biology, nutrition, cooking, consumer behavior, and every step of production from the field to the table. A master's degree in food science provides an in-depth understanding of food safety and science and qualifies holders to produce food in less typical ways. For example, a food production manager with a master's degree might focus on sustainable (environmentally friendly) methods, using organic ingredients, or harnessing renewable energy to power production machinery.

Certification

Employers expect food production managers to be certified in various food safety programs, including a program called hazard analysis critical control points (HACCP). The HACCP system is a preventive approach meant to eliminate biological, chemical, and physical hazards in the food production process.

The certified food safety HACCP manager accreditation is issued by the National Registry of Food Safety and other trade organizations. Those who receive the certification learn to conduct hazard analyses, establish safe production control methods, perform safety verification tests, and conduct continuous improvement activities. To obtain certification, candidates must pass a computer-based exam that covers the seven principles of the HACCP. The test can be taken at one of more than fifteen hundred sites in the United States and Canada.

Food production managers might also need to obtain accreditation in other areas, depending on where they work. The good manufacturing practice certification is required by the Food and Drug Administration to ensure that products meet food safety, quality, and legal requirements. The sanitation standard operating procedures certification confirms that the bearer understands the documented cleaning and sanitizing procedures required by the USDA for food production equipment, tools, and facilities.

The American Production and Inventory Control Society professional association offers the certified in production and inventory management (CPIM) credential. This designation has been shown to increase a designee's salary by 12 percent. Courses for the CPIM credential focus on management, procurement, sales and operations, master scheduling, quality control, and other production concepts. Production professionals must pass five exams to earn a CPIM designation.

Internships and Corporate Training Programs

Undergraduate and graduate students who work as interns will find they have a distinct advantage over other candidates when applying for jobs in food production facilities. Interns are given real-world experience and are presented with opportunities to learn numerous aspects of the food production business, from cleaning and maintenance to budgeting and management.

Most large food production corporations offer internships and provide information about the programs on company websites. For example, Tyson Foods offers fifty internship positions every year. Full-time interns at Tyson Foods generally work forty hours a week. Students who are attending classes work twenty hours a week.

Some companies offer corporate training programs. Kraft Heinz hosts what are called university programs, which fast-track students for major positions within the company. The company's operations trainee program pairs operations managers with trainees who are immersed in project assignments at one of the company's numerous manufacturing plants.

Skills and Personality

A typical food plant manager oversees dozens of employees as they move thousands of pounds of raw food through complex processing and packaging machinery onto pallets and trucks for distribution. A manager needs good oral and written communications skills to guarantee that the plant runs like a well-oiled machine. Managers use telephones, e-mail, and face-to-face interactions to coordinate deliveries from growers, work with safety inspectors, and lead production and safety teams. Good communication goes hand in hand with interpersonal skills—the ability to establish rapport with individuals, motivate employees, and resolve conflicts amicably.

Food production managers need to be problem solvers who can quickly identify glitches and devise ways to solve them, sometimes in an original or creative way. Innovation is another core part of a food production manager's job. Facility managers are always on the lookout for new products, processes, and equipment that can be put into service to stay ahead of competitors.

Food production managers need a solid understanding of the mechanics of food processing machines and the computers that run them. A modern food factory employs dozens of computers to monitor and control processing and packaging machinery. Food production managers work with tech teams but are ultimately responsible for controlling factory software and hardware.

On the Job

Employers

Food production managers work for companies that manufacture products ranging from cooking oils to pet food. The top-three food and beverage processing companies in the United States in 2017 were Tyson Foods, PepsiCo, and Nestlé. Other major producers include Coca-Cola, Kraft Heinz, Smithfield Foods, General Mills, and Cargill. These companies are among dozens nationwide that employ food production managers.

Working Conditions

A food production manager spends time in an office, but most days are spent on the factory floor, which is filled with dangerous equipment that slices, bakes, boils, steams, freezes, and transports heavy loads. Floors can be slippery, the air can be thick with odors, and one part of the facility can be very hot while another part is icy cold. Like all factory employees, food production managers are expected to wear safety gear like hard hats, goggles, steel-toe boots, and other equipment.

Food production managers work full time but are expected to put in overtime hours during peak production periods. Managers have many responsibilities, and the work can be stressful when deadlines are tight and problems arise.

Earnings

The Bureau of Labor Statistics (BLS) reports that all types of industrial production managers, including those who work in food manufacturing, earned a median annual salary of $97,140 in 2016. Those who are beginning their career as food production managers might start at around $60,000 annually. However, experienced food production managers who work for large corporations can earn considerably more when benefits and bonuses are included. According to the employment review website Glassdoor, food production managers employed by Tyson Foods earned a base salary of $114,417 and were awarded an average of $32,000 in cash bonuses for meeting production, budgetary, or safety criteria. Tyson food facility managers also received stock bonuses, profit sharing, medical insurance, and other benefits.

Opportunities for Advancement

Those who apply for the job of food production manager fresh out of college will likely start their careers as assistant managers who oversee one or two segments of the food production process. These managers have fewer responsibilities and proportionately lower salaries. After several years of learning on the job, workers can take over larger segments of the factory. The most successful food production professional can become a chief operating officer, an executive who oversees operations at several production facilities.

What Is the Future Outlook for Food Production Managers?

According to the BLS, employment opportunities for all industrial production managers are projected to decline by 4 percent through 2024. The bureau forecasts that automation and the continuing shift to overseas manufacturing will reduce employment in all industrial production sectors. However, food production, which heavily relies on fresh US-grown commodities, cannot be easily outsourced to foreign countries. Therefore, there will likely be less of a decline in the number of food production managers in the coming decade. Whatever the case, as long as billions of dollars' worth of food is consumed annually in the United States, there will always be employment opportunities for food production managers.

Find Out More

American Frozen Food Institute (AFFI)
2000 Corporate Ridge
McLean, VA 22102
website: www.affi.org

The AFFI is an industry trade group that offers certification for food production professionals. The institute also provides online courses in workplace safety, quality assurance, productivity, and other food manufacturing topics.

American Production and Inventory Control Society (APICS)
8430 W. Bryn Mawr Ave.
Chicago, IL 60631
website: www.apics.org

APICS is a professional association for supply chain management that provides research, education, and certification programs. The organization offers educational and training programs and issues the certified in production and inventory management credential.

Grocery Manufacturers of America (GMA)
1350 I St. NW
Washington, DC 20005
website: www.gmaonline.org

The GMA is a trade group that represents food and beverage companies. The organization underwrites the GMA Science and Education Foundation, which sponsors research projects, classroom education, mentorships, and international learning programs.

National Registry of Food Safety Professionals
6751 Forum Dr.
Orlando, FL 32821
website: www.nrfsp.com

The National Registry of Food Safety Professionals develops and maintains internationally recognized certification programs for the food safety profession. The registry is known by the food service industry for its examinations and service delivery standards and practices. Its website provides educational information, test protocols, and training information.

Food Safety Inspector

At a Glance
Food Safety Inspector

Minimum Educational Requirements

None; bachelor's degree preferred

Personal Qualities

Good observational skills, excellent communicator, record-keeping skills, bilingual, a strong stomach

Certification and Licensing

Voluntary

Working Conditions

Slaughterhouse setting, extreme temperatures, offensive odors, dangerous machinery, excessive noise

Salary

$39,000 in 2015

Number of Jobs

Approximately 32,000 in 2016

Future Job Outlook

5 percent increase for all agriculture and food science technicians through 2024

What Does a Food Safety Inspector Do?

Every year thousands of Americans get sick—and some even die—from eating tainted food. Although food-borne disease outbreaks often make headlines, the United States has one of the safest food supplies in the world. Americans collectively eat nearly a billion meals every day with relatively few problems. This is due to the work of food safety inspectors. These professionals ensure that foods produced domestically and overseas adhere to the highest standards of quality set by federal agencies.

Workers called consumer safety inspectors (CSIs) work for the Food Safety Inspection Service (FSIS), which is part of the USDA. Consumer safety inspectors at the FSIS are responsible for overseeing about 6,200 facilities, including slaughterhouses, food processing plants, and food importation businesses. Food safety inspectors also work for the Center for Food Safety and Applied Nutrition (CFSAN) within the Food and Drug Administration (FDA). Those who work for the CFSAN are responsible for inspecting over 377,000 registered food facilities—154,000 in the United States and 223,000 foreign facilities—that manufacture, process, pack, or hold food consumed by humans or animals in the United States. Food safety inspectors who work for local and state health departments are tasked with ensuring food safety at restaurants, institutional food service establishments, supermarkets, grocery stores, and other food sellers.

Food safety inspectors are trained to prevent food-borne illnesses from reaching consumers. They enforce food and health codes in manufacturing plants, meatpacking factories, and dairy and egg processing plants. The work involves comprehension of both law and science. Food safety inspectors must understand complex food handling regulations created by scientists and policy makers to protect public health. Inspectors must also grasp the science behind biological contamination to ensure that storage, handling, and processing procedures will not compromise the safety of the products being produced.

The job of the food safety inspector involves searching for contaminants or health hazards in a number of areas. They inspect food facilities, production tools, and equipment to ensure everything is clean and sanitary. Food safety inspectors check animals that are in line for slaughter to make sure they are disease-free. They review food products as they roll off production lines and ensure packages are properly labeled. Food producers are required to test raw ingredients for contaminants like *E. coli* and *Listeria,* and food safety inspectors study the test results to make sure the food is wholesome and the records are up-to-date.

Food safety inspectors also evaluate employees as they handle, prepare, and store food to ensure all processes comply with sanitation regulations. When infractions are identified, inspectors educate employees and propose actions a facility can take to avoid further problems. On the USDA website, Andrew Lino, a consumer safety inspector for the FSIS, explains the significance of the work: "Performing my duties gives me a sense of pride and comfort that I am impacting the safety of the nation's food supply in a positive manner to help prevent someone from getting sick or possibly dying. I get a sense of enjoyment and pride that I am making sure the public consumer is receiving safe, wholesome products from the establishments that I cover."

Although most food safety inspectors work in food production plants, some who work with the CFSAN travel the world to inspect foods manufactured overseas that are intended for sale in the United States. Cory Bryant is one such inspector. "More and more food is being shipped all over the world and traded between countries. It is our responsibility [at the CFSAN] to . . . enforce the regulations that will make sure that food coming into the U.S. is safe," Bryant says on the Institute of Food Technologists website. "On any given day I can be headed out to the airport to go to China for a week to carry out the duties of the FDA there. [Or] I might be . . . dealing with a new regulation to control salmonella [on foods] coming out of Kenya."

How Do You Become a Food Safety Inspector?

Education

Food safety inspectors come from various educational backgrounds. FSIS employee Rita Hurst began her career in 1984 as a poultry plant employee who assisted USDA inspectors. Although Hurst had no specific education in food inspection, she applied for a job at the FSIS and was accepted after completing the agency's Poultry Training for Food Inspectors class. Hurst, who is now a senior employee at the FSIS, credits her colleagues for shaping the course of her career. She says they helped her learn leadership and problem-solving skills that she puts to use in her job.

The FSIS continues to hire those, like Hurst, with at least one year of job-related experience in the food industry. Candidates must pass a written test and demonstrate knowledge of sanitation practices used in the handling and preparation of meat, poultry, and eggs.

Many local and state public health departments require food inspectors to hold a two-year associate's degree in animal science.

Candidates with a bachelor's degree in animal science will have broader job opportunities and earn better salaries. They will have taken advanced courses in animal biology, food science, and production management.

Certification

Although certification is not required of food safety inspectors, those who pursue official accreditation have a better chance to advance their careers. The National Environmental Health Association offers the internationally recognized certified professional–food safety (CP-FS) certification to food inspectors. The certification requires expertise in food microbiology and food inspection regulations. Those who seek CP-FS accreditation must have a bachelor's degree in food science or environmental health or any bachelor's degree with two years' experience in food safety.

Internships and Mentorships

Working in an internship program is highly recommended for students who wish to enhance their job prospects before graduating college. The FSIS offers internships in several areas. Food inspector interns work under a CSI and receive on-the-job training in sanitation procedures in slaughtering plants. The FSIS also offers mentorships with senior program investigators who examine violations of food inspection laws and ensure criminal, administrative, and civil sanctions are carried out against violators. Candidates must complete at least twelve semesters in courses such as food science, nutrition, or animal science before they apply for internships.

The FDA offers a limited number of summer, fall, and spring internships to undergraduate and graduate students through its Office of Policy. Interns work in the Office of Policy on a broad range of issues, including food safety, drug importation, disease outbreaks, and food and drug regulations. Candidates work with senior agency officials to develop professional skills and improve research techniques. Interns can apply through the FDA Office of Policy website. Upon acceptance, candidates undergo a security clearance review, including fingerprinting, a background check, and a drug test.

Skills and Personality

Food safety inspectors are literally responsible for making life-and-death decisions that can affect the health of millions of people. The job comes with great responsibility, and food safety inspectors need several skills to successfully perform their duties. As the job title implies, food safety inspectors need excellent observational skills. They need to closely examine food handling practices, equipment, and facilities, and they should be able to quickly spot problems and safety violations that pose a threat.

Food safety inspectors need to be excellent communicators. They must establish rapport with employees and gather information about the workplace. Inspectors who are bilingual or multilingual will have an advantage on the job since many workers at food processing plants are not native English speakers.

When food-handling facilities are in violation of the law, inspectors need to close the plants or revoke their business licenses. This duty requires tact and diplomacy since it is the inspector's judgment that will be responsible for people being laid off or losing their jobs.

On the Job

Employers

Food safety inspectors work for local and state government agencies. Many large cities have local inspection departments. For example, the Chicago Department of Public Health operates the Food Production Division, which maintains the safety of food bought, sold, or prepared in restaurants, grocery stores, bakeries, convenience stores, hospitals, nursing homes, day care facilities, shelters, schools, and temporary food service events. In Los Angeles, the Los Angeles County District Surveillance and Enforcement (DSE), a branch of the Department of Public Health, carries out food inspection. The DSE has twenty-nine district offices and three investigative units in Los Angeles County responsible for inspecting and enforcing public health laws at restaurants, food markets, temporary food facilities at street fairs, food warehouses, and even movie theaters. The state also runs the Inspection Services Division within the California Department of Food and

Agriculture. State inspectors oversee growers and packers to ensure that fruits, vegetables, and nuts are of good quality and are properly labeled. On the federal level, food safety inspectors work for the FSIS, the CFSAN, and the Centers for Disease Control and Prevention.

Working Conditions

It is not a joke to say that food safety inspectors need a strong stomach. The work takes place in slaughterhouses, where animals are killed and processed in ways that might sicken casual observers. The USDA warns that inspectors will be exposed to offensive odors, such as manure and blood, as they spend their workdays searching for mold, cockroaches, flies, and rats in dark corners of food production facilities. Additionally, food production facilities can be excessively cold or hot, damp, and slippery. Food safety inspectors work closely with others, around loud machinery, and with dangerous knives and other tools.

Earnings

The Bureau of Labor Statistics (BLS) does not keep separate earnings statistics for food safety inspectors. The bureau reports that all agriculture and food science technicians earned a median salary of $39,500 in 2015. However, job listings at the USDA in 2017 listed food safety inspector jobs with salaries ranging from $32,318 to $52,043 per year, with a median salary close to $42,000.

Opportunities for Advancement

Food safety inspectors who work a number of years for local and state governments can expect to be promoted to supervisory positions and managerial roles. Those who take entry level positions at the FSIS begin their careers in private commercial slaughtering plants. After gaining experience, inspectors can expect promotion to more complex operations, such as plants that produce frozen dinners. Some food safety inspectors are promoted to what are called enforcement, investigations, and analysis officers (EIAOs). These professionals inspect food safety systems in different types of commercial meat and poultry slaughtering and processing facilities. EIAOs conduct on-site scientific food safety verification activities.

What Is the Future Outlook for Food Safety Inspectors?

According to the BLS, the demand for all agriculture and food science technicians is expected to grow 5 percent through 2024. But it is likely that there will be even greater need for food safety inspectors as the population of the United States continues to grow every year and more food is produced. More food safety inspectors will be needed to keep up with growing demand.

Find Out More

Food and Drug Administration (FDA)
10903 New Hampshire Ave.
Silver Spring, MD 20993
website: www.fda.gov

The FDA oversees the bulk of all food production in the United States. The agency's website contains comprehensive information about food safety, inspector training, internship programs, and career opportunities at the Center for Food Safety and Applied Nutrition.

Food Safety Inspection Service (FSIS)
1400 Independence Ave. SW
Washington, DC 20250
website: www.fsis.usda.gov

The FSIS is a federal regulatory agency within the Department of Agriculture that is tasked with ensuring the safety of meat, poultry, and processed egg products. The service's website contains a wealth of information of interest to prospective food safety inspectors, including public health information, statistics, and employee interviews.

International Association for Food Protection (IAFP)
6200 Aurora Ave.
Des Moines, IA 50322
website: www.foodprotection.org

The IAFP is an association of food scientists, microbiologists, educators, government officials, and industry executives dedicated to protecting the global food supply. The association extends membership to students and provides educational information and student travel scholarships.

National Environmental Health Association (NEHA)
720 S. Colorado Blvd.
Denver, CO 80246
website: www.neha.org

The NEHA is a professional organization for environmental health professionals. The association provides educational resources and training through online courses and publications. The website offers certification programs for food and beverage processors and food inspectors in various fields.

Agricultural Engineer

What Does an Agricultural Engineer Do?

At a Glance
Agricultural Engineer

Minimum Educational Requirements

Bachelor's degree

Personal Qualities

Analytical, strong math skills, good communicator, problem-solving abilities

Certification and Licensing

Professional engineer license (voluntary)

Working Conditions

Indoors in offices and food production facilities and outdoors on farms and agricultural sites

Salary

$73,640 annually in 2016

Number of Jobs

2,900 in 2014

Future Job Outlook

4 percent growth through 2024

In 2017 the world's top berry grower, Driscoll's, began testing the C-3PO agricultural robot in a California strawberry field. The C-3PO utilizes digital sensors and mechanical graspers and cutters to harvest strawberries. This labor-intensive task is usually performed by agricultural workers. The strawberry harvesting robot, still in the experimental stages, is the product of agricultural engineers. These professionals use science, technology, and math to design and test machines used to plant, grow, harvest, and process food. William Brock Faulkner, an agricultural engineering professor, describes the profession in the online publication *Texas A&M AgriLife Communications*: "We produce a lot of agricultural commodities in this country. [Agricultural engineers ask] how do you harvest it, how do you transport it, how do you store it, how do you use it? . . . How do we take our raw commodities and get them to our end product with the quality and quantity that is profitable for everybody along the supply chain?"

Agricultural engineers use their skills to plan and design irrigation, drainage, and flood-control systems. They formulate plans for the construction of efficient and cost-effective agricultural buildings, grain storage facilities, food processing plants, and refrigeration systems. Agricultural engineers design new equipment and machinery that can be used to prepare fields, plant seeds, spray agricultural chemicals, harvest crops, and transport products. Some agricultural engineers specialize in feeding and waste disposal systems for dairy, poultry, and livestock facilities. Agricultural engineer Rob Menes writes on the website Quora that he relies on a broad range of scientific knowledge to perform his job: "Information technology, engineering, biology, anthropology, cartography, mathematics—they all intersect to form new ways of addressing the problems of cultivating the land, eating food, and disposing of the wastes."

Agricultural engineers interested in sustainability find ways to reduce the use of farm chemicals, eliminate air and water pollution from growing systems, and conserve water. Some design renewable energy systems, such as solar panels and windmills, that are used in farm operations. Agricultural engineers who design waste-to-energy projects create systems to convert methane gas produced by animal waste into biogas for use in electrical generation plants and machinery.

Another focus for agricultural engineers concerns what is called ag-tech, which includes technology-based systems like drones, robotics, smartphone apps, and cloud-based systems designed to make farm production more efficient. One of the most advanced projects overseen by an agricultural engineer is the 2,800-cubic-foot (79 cu. m) South Pole Food Growth Chamber (SPFGC) at the Amundsen-Scott Station in Antarctica, where temperatures hover at –100°F (–73°C) six months per year. The chamber can grow lettuce, tomatoes, cucumbers, peppers, and cantaloupe year-round for the sixty-four people who live and work at the station. The SPFGC was designed by agricultural engineers at the University of Arizona's Controlled Environment Agriculture Program, and the project is intended to provide

NASA with information that the space agency can use to someday grow food in hostile environments on the Moon and Mars.

How Do You Become an Agricultural Engineer?

Education

A bachelor of science degree in agricultural engineering is a basic requirement for anyone wishing to become an agricultural engineer. In 2017 there were fifteen colleges in the United States that specifically offered this degree. These schools are certified by the Accreditation Board for Engineering and Technology (ABET), which provides assurance that the institution meets the quality standards of the engineering profession.

Most students studying for a bachelor's degree in agricultural engineering work toward a standard engineering degree with a focus on agriculture, land planning, or geographic information systems. Courses focus on many aspects of the agriculture industry, including tractors and power units, systems analysis in agriculture, food processing engineering technology, water and soil management, occupational safety management, processing and storage of agricultural products, aquaculture (seafood farming), electronics and control systems, and information technology for agricultural systems. Students combine classroom studies with laboratory projects and hands-on fieldwork. Some who major in agricultural science will minor in related topics, such as food science or economics. Most colleges and universities encourage students to gain experience by participating in engineering competitions in which teams of students design equipment and attempt to solve real-world problems.

Those who go on to pursue a master's degree in agricultural engineering learn to solve problems through science and technology. They study food engineering; environmental and natural resource engineering; machine and energy systems; systems analysis; and food, feed, and fiber processing. Some go on to obtain a doctorate in agricultural engineering, which gives them the background to conduct independent research.

Licensing

Although it is not required for an entry-level position, some agricultural engineers choose to become licensed professional engineers (PEs). Professional engineers garner higher salaries and advanced positions of leadership. A PE license allows the holder to oversee the work of other engineers, give final approval to projects, and provide services directly to the public (as opposed to working for a company or an engineering firm).

Those who wish to become PEs need a degree from an ABET-accredited engineering program and must pass two exams. Recent graduates who have earned their bachelor's degree in agricultural engineering can take the computer-based Fundamentals of Engineering Exam, which includes 110 questions that must be answered within six hours. Those who pass the exam are called engineers in training or engineer interns. After at least four years of relevant work experience, candidates take a second exam, called the Principles and Practice of Engineering. The exam contains 80 multiple-choice questions and is administered over the course of eight hours.

Internships

Most students who major in agricultural engineering spend time working as interns. Major agriculture corporations offer numerous internship positions on company websites, and undergraduate and graduate students are encouraged to apply. For example, the agricultural commodities company Cargill provides engineering students with the opportunity to apply their classroom knowledge to a food processing business environment at various plants across the country. Agricultural engineer interns at Cargill gain an understanding of plant processes and equipment, energy issues, and production efficiencies.

Colleges and universities offer internships in research labs. On the Michigan State University website, agricultural engineer Mike Zanotti recalls his four-month internship at the university's biofuels research lab during his junior year in 2011:

> Working for . . . [the biofuels lab] has been the high-
> light of my time here at Michigan State. I was able to

gain a much deeper understanding of the issues surrounding the biofuels industry, something that my courses could only scratch the surface of. My time as a research assistant cemented my commitment to continue my education into graduate school, which, before this experience I had not really given much thought to."

Skills and Personality

As with other tech and science-related careers, agricultural engineers need to be good analysts. They must understand the workings of complex agricultural and food production systems and devise ways to improve these systems. The work involves analyzing workers, equipment, tools, and the environment. Agricultural engineers need highly developed problem-solving skills to address issues concerning safety, efficiency, and systems management. They rely on calculus, trigonometry, and other advanced mathematical skills to design, analyze, and troubleshoot. Engineering projects require teamwork, and agricultural engineers need to possess good speaking and listening skills to communicate with clients, supervisors, workers, and others.

Agricultural engineers who work in farm and food processing settings must be in good physical shape. The job sometimes requires bending, squatting, reaching, working on irregular surfaces, and the occasional lifting of objects weighing over 50 pounds (23 kg).

On the Job

Employers

Agricultural engineers work for food processors, agricultural equipment manufacturers, seed and chemical companies, agribusiness research facilities, construction companies, biofuel producers, and government agencies like NASA and the US Department of Energy. Major corporations that hire agricultural engineers include 3M, Archer Daniels Midland, BASF, Caterpillar, ExxonMobil, Raytheon, the Ford Motor Company, Nestlé Purina, John Deere, Lockheed Martin, and Monsanto.

Working Conditions

Agricultural engineers usually work full time, but they may have to work overtime when deadlines loom or projects run into unexpected problems. They spend most of their time in offices, where they use computer-aided design (CAD) software to create plans and blueprints for machinery and building projects. Continuing education is part of the job, and agricultural engineers spend time reviewing research and reading books and articles on the latest developments in their industry. They also deal with bureaucratic tasks, such as managing budgets, preparing and presenting technical reports to clients and supervisors, and coordinating with zoning boards and other government regulators.

Some agricultural engineers work in laboratories conducting research, and some work outdoors overseeing the construction of farm and food processing systems. They often visit clients to analyze problems, study plant layouts, and help train workers.

Earnings

In 2016 the median annual wage for agricultural engineers was $73,640. The median wage is the wage at which half the workers earned more and half earned less. The lowest-paid 10 percent of agricultural engineers earned less than $45,510, and the highest-paid 10 percent earned more than $117,130. Agricultural engineers who worked for engineering firms had the highest salaries, with an average salary of $98,360. Those who were employed by the federal government brought in around $81,500, and agricultural engineers in the food manufacturing industry earned $77,900. Colleges and universities paid lower wages to professors of agricultural engineering; they earned a median salary of $54,610.

Opportunities for Advancement

Entry-level agricultural engineers generally work under the supervision of experienced engineers. As they gain knowledge and experience, they are given more responsibilities and independence to solve problems. They may take over difficult projects and develop their own design solutions. As their careers advance, agricultural engineers might supervise teams of engineers or become managers of a department or entire firm. Some go into sales; in this capacity, their job entails explaining to clients the technical and engineering aspects of the employer's products. Salespeople can earn large commissions when sales are completed.

What Is the Future for Agricultural Engineers?

The Bureau of Labor Statistics (BLS) forecasts that the demand for agricultural engineers will grow by 4 percent through 2024. The BLS also notes that the range of cutting-edge projects in sectors such as biofuels, automated farming technologies, and even space-based food production will provide a growing demand for agricultural engineers. Additionally, strong global competition will pressure farmers to find better and more efficient ways to grow crops, which bodes well for the employment prospects of agricultural engineers. Faulkner is optimistic about the future of this career: "This is a fun place to be. . . . Agricultural engineering is going to be one of the most in-demand professions as we go forward. We're trying to feed a growing population with limited resources. We're trying to provide clothes; we're trying to provide fuel. There are tons of opportunities out there."

Find Out More

Accreditation Board for Engineering and Technology (ABET)
415 N. Charles St.
Baltimore, MD 21201
website: www.abet.org

The ABET accredits college and university programs that teach applied science, computing, engineering, and engineering technology at the associate's, bachelor's, and master's degree levels. The organization hosts events, workshops, and webinars, and the ABET website offers students a national list of ABET-accredited programs.

American Society of Agricultural and Biological Engineers (ASABE)
2950 Niles Rd.
St. Joseph, MO 49085
website: www.asabe.org

The ASABE is an international society of professionals focused on the advancement of engineering related to agriculture, food, and biological systems. The website provides continuing education and career development information, and the ASABE Foundation offers student awards and scholarships.

Engineers Without Borders
1031 Thirty-Third St., Suite 210
Denver, CO 80205
website: www.ewb-usa.org

Engineers Without Borders is dedicated to improving the lives of people through engineering projects that allow communities to meet their basic human needs and equipping leaders to solve the world's most pressing challenges. The group offers educational opportunities to those interested in managing engineering projects domestically and internationally.

Society of Women Engineers (SWE)
203 N. La Salle St., Suite 1675
Chicago, IL 60601
website: http://societyofwomenengineers.swe.org

The SWE is dedicated to giving women engineers a unique voice within the engineering field. The organization runs an outreach program for students in kindergarten through twelfth grade, provides scholarships to female students, and sponsors individual and collegiate competitions and awards.

Baker

According to a study by the National Academy of Sciences, prehistoric people in Europe first made bread around thirty thousand years ago. Since that time the need for daily bread has played a central role in the development of agriculture and modern civilization itself. As baker Rick Easton says about bread on the Persephone Bakery website, "It's the most basic and essential way of feeding someone. Bread [is] this absolute necessity, this staple foodstuff. And it's pure. And it's simple."

Today the baking industry generates more than $102 billion annually and employs thousands of people who bake loaves of bread and other goods, including crackers, cakes, pastries, pies, scones, muffins, rolls, and tortillas. Those who work as bakers have different duties than professional cooks or chefs. According to an old adage among culinary professionals, cooking is an art while baking is a science. Chefs tend to experiment and improvise, adding new ingredients or changing recipes to highlight different flavors. Bakers need to be precise and follow recipes exactly. If too little yeast and

At a Glance

Baker

Minimum Educational Requirements
None

Personal Qualities
Early riser, detail oriented, good communicator, physically fit

Certification and Licensing
Voluntary

Working Conditions
Indoors in hot kitchens and cold freezers; ten-hour workdays, six days a week

Salary
$25,090 annually in 2016

Number of Jobs
185,300 in 2014

Future Job Outlook
7 percent growth through 2024

A baker adds icing to her freshly baked pastries. Bakers must have a thorough understanding of chemistry, and must also be willing to rise early in the morning and remain on their feet for hours at a time.

sugar is added, bread will not rise. If too much liquid is added to a brownie recipe, the final product ends up a soupy mess destined for the garbage can. As bakery owner Carolina Garofani writes on the website Quora, "You get to do a lot of research, [act like a] scientist, and learn more about the chemistry and physics involved in pastry—it's a LOT, and I'm a total nerd."

Flour is the main ingredient of the baker's craft—and the foundation of almost all baked goods—along with sugar, yeast, and eggs. Bakers spend their workdays kneading, rolling, cutting, and shaping dough and applying glazes, icings, and other toppings to dessert goods. They use measuring cups and spoons, bowls, scales, blenders, mixers, and ovens to produce baked goods. Their products are sold by grocers, wholesalers, restaurants, and institutional food services.

Some professional bakers work for commercial bakeries, where they operate high-volume mixing machines and automated baking equipment. Every day commercial bakeries create an established list of breads, pastries, and baked goods. Other bakers work in retail establishments like grocery stores, bakeries, specialty shops, and restaurants, where they make fresh-baked products that are sold directly to consumers or are eaten on-site. Because retail bakers work on a smaller scale, they have the option of producing a wider range of flavors and products. For example, retail bakers who work at artisan bread shops might bake a dozen different types of bread, from sourdough to jalapeño cheddar.

Those who work in commercial bakeries make huge volumes of bread dough, cookie dough, and cake batter and oversee numerous workers who help with cookie cutting, cake assembly, bread loaf shaping, baking, decorating, and packaging. Most commercial bakeries operate with a very low profit margin, earning only a few cents on each product. This means commercial bakers are under pressure to work as quickly and efficiently as possible.

In addition to baking, bakers spend a good amount of time cleaning. Hygiene is extremely important in a kitchen. After every round of baking, bakers work hard at cleaning floors and sanitizing counters, utensils, and other equipment. And after the baking is finished for the day, the baker will clean the kitchen once again and then spend a few hours preparing ingredients and products for the next morning.

Whether the baker works in a large commercial facility or a small artisan bakery, the job can be very demanding. "You're standing up for 10 to 12 hours a day," says Garofani. "Your back hurts, your knees hurt, your hair always feels oily and dirty . . . and every day is a crazy rush in a whirlwind of flour, sugar and chocolate powder. You make up to 60 recipes a day. Sometimes you do the same thing for hours, like making 1,200 cookies." But Garofani adds that baking provides her with great personal satisfaction: "Feedback is amazing, people come back wanting more, and seeing the finished product is so gratifying. . . . A lot of love and a lot of sugar. I definitely love what I do!"

How Do You Become a Baker?

Education

There are no formal educational requirements to become a baker, but a high school diploma makes a job candidate more attractive to most employers. High school teaches basic reading, math, and science skills that are necessary to follow recipes, calculate weights and measures, and carry out essential baking concepts. While in high school, a potential baker should focus on elective courses like home economics and cooking. Beyond a high school diploma, most employers at commercial bakeries and small retail bakeries are interested in previous experience. Job candidates can improve their employment prospects by working part-time or at summer jobs in supermarkets, restaurants, or bakeries.

Although most bakers learn their skills through on-the-job training, those who wish to produce fancy baked products, like artisan breads, high-end pastries, or wedding cakes, attend culinary school. These institutions offer one- or two-year courses that cover every aspect of baking, cake decoration, health and sanitation practices, and baking economics. Culinary schools are expensive, however, and they leave most students saddled with debt. Those hoping to avoid debt can take baking classes offered by cookware stores, bread shops, and other institutions.

Certification

Although bakers are not required to have any specific accreditation, those who seek voluntary certification show employers that they have the skills and knowledge to properly perform their duties. The Retail Bakers of America offers certification at a variety of levels. Those holding a certified baker accreditation are skilled in a broad range of commercial bakery operations, including staff management, budgets, and retail sales and merchandising. A certified decorator accreditation can be obtained by bakers who are experts at finishing sweet baked goods, preparing icings, and decorating cakes. Bakers at the level of certified master baker understand a broad range of complex, technical, and professional baking activities, including administrative skills and the principles of sanitation, management, and training.

Requirements for certification vary. A certified baker must have four years of work experience and thirty hours of sanitation course work. A certified master baker must have eight years of work experience, thirty hours of sanitation course work, and thirty hours of professional development education.

Internships and Apprenticeships

Perhaps the fastest way to learn the baker's business is to apply for an internship at an establishment that produces baked goods. Qualifications vary from one institution to the next, but many who hire interns expect candidates to have attended culinary school or to have work experience. Some require a portfolio consisting of photographs of baked goods produced by the candidate. Candidates might be able to use their internships toward school credit.

Many bakers learn their trade working as a baker's apprentice at a grocery store or bakery for one to three years. Apprentices are taught to read and understand recipes, prepare baked goods, knead and cut bread dough, operate bakery equipment, and train assistants. Apprentices also work in customer service, helping with sales and taking phone orders.

Skills and Personality

Customers expect cakes to be flawlessly decorated and loaves of bread to be perfectly shaped. This requires bakers to be detail oriented to produce products that not only taste good but look picture perfect. Bakers also need to follow the details of a recipe without fail, which requires strong basic math skills. Bakers work with teaspoons, tablespoons, cups, and pounds, and they must be able to multiply and divide these measurements. They need to understand weights, volumes, and fractions to mix and weigh ingredients using addition, subtraction, and multiplication.

The job also requires good physical health. Bakers have to be strong enough to lift sacks of flour and sugar, which can weigh 50 to 100 pounds (23 to 45 kg). Bakers also move around large, heavy baking sheets filled with cookies and other baked goods.

Bakers are required to work quickly and accurately with assistants, other bakers, customers, and the occasional health inspector. This makes good people skills a must. On the Persephone Bakery website, Easton poetically offers a few more helpful traits: "There's a lot of lessons to be learned [from baking] bread. It takes sensitivity. It takes vigilance. It takes discipline. [It takes] focus. It takes care. And I think these are all qualities that I hope I express in my daily life."

On the Job

Employers

Bakers work in retail bakeries, large commercial bakeries, tortilla manufacturing facilities, grocery stores, restaurants, and other eating establishments. The largest bakery company in the United States is Bimbo Bakeries, which produces many of the leading brands of baked goods found on grocer's shelves, including Entenmann's, Sara Lee, Brownberry, and Thomas. About 40 percent of all bakers worked for grocery stores in 2014 (the last year for which statistics were available). These grocers included national chains like SuperValu, Trader Joe's, and Whole Foods. Some bakers are self-employed. They run home-based bakeries and sell their products directly to their neighbors, in local shops, or at farmer's markets. Some specialize in wedding cakes, and others focus on cupcakes or pies.

Working Conditions

Bakers often work fifty to sixty hours per week, including very early mornings, late evenings, weekends, and holidays. One positive aspect of mass-producing baked goods is that there is usually plenty of free food as well as scraps and leftovers.

In addition to long hours, bakers have to be careful when moving between oven-heated kitchens and freezers where ingredients and products are stored. The sudden change in temperature between extreme hot and cold can have an adverse effect on the body for some, which might include respiratory and vascular problems. Additionally, kitchens are dangerous; hot cookie sheets, sharp knives, and industrial baking equipment can cause cuts, burns, and mangled limbs, and slippery floors can cause slips and falls.

Earnings

Bakers might make a lot of dough, but they do not make a lot of money. According to the Bureau of Labor Statistics (BLS), bakers earned a median annual wage of $25,090 in 2016. The median wage is the wage at which half the workers earned more and half earned less. The lowest-paid 10 percent of bakers earned less than $18,640, while the highest-paid 10 percent earned more than $39,050.

Opportunities for Advancement

Bakers might start out as entry-level assistants and earn promotions to become bakers. Those with years of experience, especially in producing specialty products, can become plant managers at large bakeries or even move into executive positions, overseeing a number of bakeries owned by their employer.

What Is the Future Outlook for Bakers?

Americans love bread and other baked goods, and the population of the country continues to grow. This bodes well for future job opportunities for bakers. However, according to the BLS, bakeries will increasingly replace their bakers with automated baking machines and other equipment in the coming years. Regardless, the BLS says employment of bakers is projected to grow 7 percent through 2024, about as fast as the average for all occupations.

Find Out More

American Bakers Association (ABA)
1300 I St. NW
Washington, DC 20005
website: www.americanbakers.org

The American Bakers Association is a baking industry trade group that sponsors the Cookie & Cracker Academy (CCA). The CCA offers three training programs, including the Entry Level Training Program, the Intermediate Training Course, and the Cookie & Cracker Manufacturing Course.

American Culinary Federation (ACF)
180 Center Place Way
St. Augustine, FL 32095
website: www.acfchefs.org

The American Culinary Federation offers educational and training resources, career advice, apprenticeship programs, and certification for current and future chefs. The Young Chefs Club is open to ACF members between the ages of sixteen and twenty-five.

American Institute of Baking (AIB)
PO Box 3999
Manhattan, KS 66505
website: www.aibonline.org

The AIB is a technical and educational organization that offers training, career development, job listings, and other information to bakers and prospective bakers.

Retail Bakers of America (RBA)
15941 Harlem Ave.
Tinley Park, IL 60477
website: www.retailbakersofamerica.org

The RBA is dedicated to promoting a profitable baking industry through training programs, information exchanges, mentorships, and networking. The RBA's certification program offers four levels of accreditation for baking professionals.

Craft Brewer

What Does a Craft Brewer Do?

Brewing beer is one of the oldest industrial processes known to humanity—the workers who built the Great Pyramids of Giza in Egypt were paid in beer. Today the United States is home to more than fifty-three hundred breweries, more than at any other time in the country's history. That number astounds industry experts. In 1980 there were only one hundred breweries in America, and in 2008 there were fifteen hundred. By 2014 the craft brewing industry was contributing $55.7 billion to the US economy, according to the Brewers Association trade group. By 2016 two new breweries were opening every day. With numbers like that, it is safe to say that the craft brewing business is one of the fastest-growing sectors of the beverage production economy.

Around 99 percent of all American breweries are craft breweries, which can be classified as either brewpubs or microbreweries. Brewpubs are restaurant-breweries that serve food and make beer on the premises. Microbreweries

---

At a Glance

Craft Brewer

Minimum Educational Requirements

None

Personal Qualities

Scientifically and mechanically inclined, physically fit, good math skills, cooking abilities

Certification and Licensing

Voluntary; brewers need to be at least twenty-one years old

Working Conditions

Brewers work long days scrubbing, bending, climbing, standing, and lifting in hot, humid breweries

Salary

$62,500 average annual salary in 2015

Number of Jobs

Around 15,000 in 2017

Future Job Outlook

6 percent growth through 2025

---

are beer factories where beer is brewed and put in bottles, cans, or kegs for sale in taverns, liquor shops, supermarkets, and other stores. Whether the facility is a warehouse microbrewery or an upmarket brewpub, beer-making professionals called craft brewers, sometimes called brewmasters or head brewers, participate in every step of the beer-making process.

Most craft beer is made from four basic ingredients: water, yeast, barley, and hops, which are the flowers of the hop plant. (Sometimes wheat, rye, or fruits are added to the mix.) Craft brewers oversee the scientific process called malting that turns the starch in grain into various sugars. These sugars feed the yeast, which converts the sugar into alcohol and carbon dioxide, or beer bubbles. Hops work as a

A craft brewer works on his brewery's staple IPA beer. Craft brewers must have an understanding of the many different types of hops, malt, and beer yeast, as they oversee the many stages of beer production.

preservative and flavoring agent, giving beer a desirable bitterness that balances out the sweetness of the malt.

This seemingly simple process can be used to make dozens of different beer styles, such as pilsners, lagers, porters, bocks, and pale ales. Craft brewers need to understand the many different types of hops, malt, and beer yeast that make up each style. For example, a porter gets its brown color from the type of dark malt used in the brewing process, and its extra bitterness comes from the type of hops added during the brewing process. In addition to understanding traditional recipes, craft brewers are expected to use their artistic flair to invent their own versions of each style, differentiating their beers from hundreds of others brewed by competitors.

Throughout the brewing process, the craft brewer controls a massive copper and stainless steel brewing system. On a typical brewing day, a craft brewer adds crushed barley to hot water in a giant gas-fired cooking vessel called a mash tun. The barley, which looks like a giant bowl of oatmeal, is held at various temperatures for specific periods of time to create a sweet substance called mash. The mash is fed into a giant strainer called a lauter tun, which separates the liquid from the grain. The liquid, called wort, is transferred to a brew kettle, where it is boiled for an hour or more. The craft brewer adds hops at various stages of the process. The wort is cooled down, the brewer adds the yeast, and the liquid ferments over the course of several weeks. The fermented beer is then moved to conditioning tanks to clarify and age for a month or more.

Although cooking up batches of beer is fun, there is an old saying among craft brewers that 80 percent of brewing is cleaning. Craft brewers clean before making beer, during the brewing process, and after the batch is tanked. Warm wort and yeast attract all sorts of invisible bacteria and other microbes that can adversely affect the taste, smell, and quality of beer. A batch of bad beer goes down the drain, costing the brewery thousands of dollars. For that reason, craft brewers spend most of their days in rubber boots, gloves, aprons, and goggles while working with detergents and sanitizers formulated to kill living organisms that thrive in brewery equipment. Brewers jump into mash tuns with chemicals and scrub brushes, circulate sanitizers through hoses and lines that connect equipment, and pay extra attention to valves and fittings where bacteria can build up.

While craft brewers at brewpubs or larger microbreweries spend all their time brewing and cleaning, those who work for smaller microbreweries might also be in charge of transferring beer into bottles, cans, or steel kegs. This requires knowledge of various machines that consist of fillers, cappers, labelers, and conveyors. During bottling operations, craft brewers might be required to load heavy cases of beer onto pallets.

Craft brewers also deal with paperwork and bureaucracy. Brewing is regulated at the federal level by the Bureau of Alcohol, Tobacco, Firearms, and Explosives. Craft brewers are required to fill out reports every two weeks that provide details about the exact number of barrels produced and the amount of beer that is spilled or wasted during operations. Additional paperwork is required by states, which also tax beer production.

How Do You Become a Craft Brewer?

Education

Many craft brewers begin their careers as home brewers. As beer journalist Chris Morris writes in 2015 in *Fortune*, "Most craft breweries started in the kitchen. Beer lovers . . . decided to try their hand at making their own—and it became popular enough amongst friends that they rolled the dice and opened a brewery of their own."

Almost every city and town has a home brew club with members who share information, tips, and recipes. Many have home brew competitions judged by local craft brewers, and winners can sometimes leverage a win into a full-time job at a brewery. However, with the continued growth of the craft beer industry, owners and managers of microbreweries and brewpubs are less inclined to hire untrained brewing staff. Most prefer employees who have a good understanding of brewing science, engineering, and brewery operations.

Those who wish to enhance the odds of landing a job as a craft brewer can attend one of the numerous schools listed on the Brewers Association website. The most respected institutions include the American Society of Brewing Chemists in St. Paul, Minnesota, and the Siebel Institute of Technology & World Brewing Academy in Chicago. There are also numerous university-affiliated programs offered at institutions throughout the United States, Canada, Germany, and the United Kingdom.

Certification

As with most professions, certification helps craft brewers enhance their job prospects and earn higher salaries. In 2017 brewers who attended a ten-week course offered by the extension program of the University of California–Davis, paid $9,800 to earn a professional brewers' certification. The certificate shows that the holder is qualified to select raw ingredients, produce wort, manage the yeast and fermentation processes, and package the product to the highest standards of the brewing industry.

Volunteer Work and Internships

Prospective brewers often start their careers as volunteers or interns. Craft brewers jokingly refer to this type of labor as working in the rat cellar, which refers to previous centuries when barrels and other supplies were kept in a brewery's basement. Cellar rats, as these volunteers and interns are called, perform a lot of cleaning and sanitation; they scrub floors, sterilize equipment, and wash empty kegs before they are refilled. Cellar rats are also expected to offload sacks of grain from trucks, work on bottling lines, and perform other tough physical jobs. Anyone interested in such a position can inquire about opportunities at local breweries.

Skills and Personality

Craft brewers draw on a combination of creativity, scientific knowledge, and hard physical work. They are passionate about beer and brewing, are attuned to the subtle flavor profiles of various brews, and are knowledgeable about the methods and processes used to create each style. Brewers must know how to use scientific instruments to measure bitterness, yeast viability, color, and other factors. They need to be mechanically inclined to operate industrial brewing equipment, and they must be in good shape to engage in the hard physical work of making beer.

On the Job

Employers

Craft brewers work at microbreweries, which are defined by the Brewers Association as breweries that make less than 15,000 barrels annually and sell 75 percent or more of their beer off-site. Craft brewers also work at brewpubs, which sell most of their beer on-site, often dispensed directly from the brewery's storage tanks. Craft brewers can also be found working at regional breweries with an annual beer production of between 15,000 and 6 million barrels. Regional breweries tend to be older facilities, like the Jacob Leinenkugel Brewing Company in Chippewa Falls, Wisconsin. This brewery has been making beer for more than a century and has traditionally sold its products in the Upper Midwest. Some regional breweries, like the Sierra Nevada Brewing Company in Chico, California, started out as microbreweries but expanded production over the years as their beers became more popular.

Working Conditions

The brewing process takes ten hours from start to finish, and brewers are on their feet the entire time, working in conditions that are often hot, humid, and slippery. Brewers clean with harsh chemicals, climb on platforms, scale ladders connected to brewing equipment, and regularly lift 50-pound (23 kg) sacks of grain. Brewers also tend to drink a lot of beer, which can cause obesity and numerous other health problems.

Earnings

The Bureau of Labor Statistics does not keep figures on the number of craft brewers in the United States, nor their salaries. However, the Craft Beverage Jobs website says that assistant brewers earn between $25,000 and $40,000 annually, and head brewers can make between $45,000 and $80,000 a year.

Opportunities for Advancement

Many professional brewers start their careers as home brewers. They begin with entry-level jobs, such as assistant brewer, and eventually become master brewers who oversee all brewery operations. And many craft brewers use their industry connections to raise money from investors and open their own breweries. On the West Coaster website, Andrew Heino, the owner of the San Diego Pacific Brewing Company, describes his career trajectory:

> [I was] homebrewing non-stop for 10 years. I started out as a volunteer at Oceanside Ale Works, then got hired on at Stone Brewing [in Escondido, California] as their first assistant brewer. I worked in various positions there, learning every day and becoming more and more knowledgeable. I decided to start my own brewery about eight years ago and I've never looked back.

What Is the Future Outlook for Craft Brewers?

According to the Motley Fool, a financial services website, for years the craft brewing industry exhibited double-digit growth rates, but it slowed to single-digit growth in 2016. Even with that slowdown, the industry is growing at about 6 percent a year. With two craft breweries opening every day on average, the future looks bright for those who want to spend their workdays brewing beer.

Find Out More

American Brewers Guild (ABG)
1001 Maple St.
Salisbury, VT 05769
website: www.abgbrew.com

The ABG is a brewing school that offers on-site classroom instruction as well as two correspondence courses: the Intensive Brewing Science and

Engineering course and the CraftBrewers Apprenticeship Program. The guild offers employment services and other career development information.

American Society of Brewing Chemists (ASBC)
3340 Pilot Knob Rd.
St. Paul, MN 55121
website: www.asbcnet.org

The ASBC is a scientific organization that represents large and small breweries. The society's website provides scholarship information and career advice for brewers and brewing specialists.

Brewers Association (BA)
1327 Spruce St.
Boulder, CO 80302
website: www.brewersassociation.org

The Brewers Association is a trade organization that represents the craft beer industry. The BA website provides numerous resources for prospective brewers, with links to industry statistics, career resources, brewing publications, and brewing schools and organizations.

Siebel Institute of Technology & World Brewing Academy
900 N. Branch St.
Chicago, IL 60642
website: www.siebelinstitute.com

This respected beer research institution was founded in 1868 to promote brewing investigation, analysis, and instruction. The website provides extensive information about the World Brewing Academy's campus-based and online brewing courses, certification, and continuing education.

Food Scientist

What Does a Food Scientist Do?

Walk through a typical supermarket and you will see aisle after aisle of products that did not exist ten—or even five—years ago. Gluten-free breakfast cereals, incredibly spicy ghost pepper potato chips, and ketchup containing bits of onion and bacon. These offerings are among some of the ten thousand new food products introduced every year. Although hungry consumers probably never give it a thought, this wave of new products would not exist without the work of food scientists. Food scientists use chemistry, engineering, microbiology, consumer research, and other skills to develop, create, and market new food products.

Food scientists work with more than five thousand food additives approved by the FDA. These additives include flavor enhancers, artificial colors, vitamins, stabilizers, and preservatives. They can be found in a wide range of processed foods, including canned goods, frozen dinners, beverages, cereals, lunch meats, sweet and salty snacks—even yogurt. Without food science, many of America's favorite foods would not exist, or they would look bad,

At a Glance
Food Scientist

Minimum Educational Requirements
Bachelor's degree in food science

Personal Qualities
Science, chemistry, math, and communication skills; good at data analysis and scientific observation

Certification and Licensing
Voluntary

Working Conditions
Full-time work in offices, labs, and food production facilities

Salary
$63,950 median annual salary in 2016

Number of Jobs
36,100 in 2014

Future Job Outlook
5 percent growth rate through 2024

taste bland, attract mold, or disintegrate into piles of crumbs.

Michael Nestrud, a sensory scientist with a doctorate in food science, explains his work in a career spotlight interview on the *Lifehacker* blog: "[When] we're creating . . . new products, the consumer is involved early and often. Through lengthy taste tests and questionnaires with tens or hundreds of people, and either at central facilities or in peoples' homes, we are the communication [line] between consumers and our product developers and marketers."

Food scientists are guided by a five-step process known as the five Ds, developed by the Institute of Food Technologists (IFT), a professional association of food scientists. The five Ds stand for *decide, discover, define, develop*, and *deploy*. In 2016 food scientists at the snack food producer Mondelez International developed a successful new brand, Véa crackers, using the five Ds. The food scientists began their work by focusing on the first two Ds, *decide* and *discover*. They conducted detailed statistical research and analysis to decide what type of new product to develop.

During the decide-and-discover phase, Mondelez employed professionals called sensory scientists. These food scientists focus on the way food tastes, smells, appears, feels, and even sounds when bitten into. The sensory scientists formed test groups with hundreds of consumers of various ages and economic backgrounds. The consumers were interviewed and fed around twenty different cracker prototypes, which they were asked to rate. The sensory scientists discovered that 80 percent of the millennials (people born between the early 1980s and the early 2000s) enjoyed cracker ingredients that originated with other cultures. Using this research, the sensory scientists decided to develop cracker flavors using Greek hummus, Mexican garden herbs, and Peruvian sweet potatoes.

Using the information gleaned from consumers, Mondelez food scientists went to work in laboratory test kitchens to define and develop the product. Research showed that millennials prefer foods that do not contain preservatives or artificial colors and flavors. This information led the food scientists to create crackers without artificial flavors or colors. The brand was defined by natural ingredients, including cayenne pepper, sunflower seeds, butternut squash, black beans, and the ancient grain quinoa.

Once the product was created, food scientists who specialize in packaging worked to deploy, or market, the product in colorful stand-up pouches. The packages were functional; they were designed to ensure that the crackers remained fresh and flavorful. Scientists were also involved in creating and designing the labels; the federal government publishes over one thousand pages of complex rules for labels. They must inform consumers about a food's ingredients and nutritional value, how the food is produced, and so on. Beyond the technical requirements, the bright, attractive labels highlighted terms like *natural* and *no artificial flavors*.

The Véa crackers were an instant success, generating over $70 million for Mondelez in the first six months of 2017. The story of the crackers shows how food scientists are utilized in nearly every aspect of bringing a product to market. But not all food scientists are responsible for making crackers taste like hummus and herbs. According to the IFT website, "Food science professionals meet a basic human need—ensuring a safe, abundant, nutritious, and flavorful food supply for the world." Some develop foods that have a higher nutritional or vitamin content. Others work to discover new food sources that are healthier or better for the environment when produced. Food scientists also conduct research to make foods that resist deadly microbes so they can be sold in developing nations to feed malnourished people.

How Do You Become a Food Scientist?

Education

Prospective food scientists should take as many science classes as they can in high school. After graduating from high school, students need to obtain a bachelor of science degree in either food science or food science and technology. Schools that offer these specific degrees are accredited through the IFT. Courses focus on core sciences, including food chemistry, food engineering, food microbiology, food analysis, food processing, and sensory and consumer sciences. Other course work might include biotechnology, culinary arts, nutritional science, agricultural economics, packaging and distribution, and food quality control and management. Students also learn business fundamentals, statistical analysis methods, and computer courses.

A master's degree in food science, food microbiology, food chemistry, or food engineering is required for those who wish to conduct research or assume duties as managers and administrators at food production companies. The IFT publishes a comprehensive list of universities with relevant graduate programs. Master's degree programs require students to complete additional classroom work, participate in fieldwork, and write a thesis based on independent research.

Those who obtain a doctorate in food science are qualified to work as project leaders, company directors, and professors. Doctoral programs emphasize original research that culminates with the writing and presentation of a dissertation.

Certification and Licensing

Food science professionals often seek certification to advance to supervisory roles. Certification can be obtained through a number of organizations. The Research Chefs Association offers a certified culinary scientist accreditation to food scientists who have first studied the culinary arts with the goal of developing unique food products. Food scientists can also obtain a hazard analysis critical control points (HACCP) auditor certification, an FDA food safety standard offered by the American Society for Quality.

The IFT offers a certified food scientist credential. Its ten-hour prep course, which cost $760 in 2017, includes online video presentations, practice tests, and a final exam. The course covers subjects such as food chemistry, analysis, microbiology, engineering and product development, food safety, and sensory evaluation.

Internships

Internships are a great way for prospective food scientists to gain work experience and develop contacts in the food production industry. Nearly every government agency, food processor, and food packager has a career link on its website with details about internship programs. The Department of Food Science and Human Nutrition at Michigan State University provides a list of companies where food science majors can apply for internships. The list includes major food companies, including the H.J. Heinz Company, the Quaker Oats Company, Borden, General Mills, the Hershey Company, the Kellogg Company, Tyson Foods, and Mars, Inc.

Some colleges and universities pair interns with food industry entities. Jonathan Deutsch, a professor of food science at Drexel University in Philadelphia, describes his school's program on the Specialty Food Association website:

> Because we have . . . food science programs, undergraduate and graduate, at a university, we're often asked to work with the industry, government, and nonprofits to help them tackle real world problems. We started the food lab a few years ago [which] . . . gives students an opportunity to work side-by-side with industry professionals during their schooling so that when they're ready to graduate, they already have great contacts and experience.

Skills and Personality

As the job title implies, food scientists must be good at science, including food microbiology, food chemistry, food engineering, botany, and nutrition. Food scientists need to be team players who can work with average shoppers, production workers, technicians, managers, and chief executive officers. They need good communications skills to clearly explain their methods, research, and findings. Food scientists must excel in critical thinking skills so they can determine the best ways to turn consumer surveys, flavor profiles, and various ingredients into edible food products. Like their colleagues in other fields, food scientists must have highly developed math, computer, and observational skills.

On the Job

Employers

Food scientists work wherever foods are created or regulated. Some work for government agencies like the FDA or the USDA where they regulate food ingredients, processing, and handling methods. Government food scientists use research to write rules and regulations meant to ensure food safety and quality. Food scientists also work for commercial food manufacturing companies, where they conduct research into and development of new products. Likewise, colleges and universities hire food scientists to teach and conduct research.

Working Conditions

Food scientists generally work forty hours a week; if deadlines for new products are looming, they might work up to sixty hours a week. Depending on their place of employment, food scientists spend their days performing research in laboratories, reading reports in offices, and conducting fieldwork where food is produced. Food processing plants are filled with dangerous, loud machinery and can be extremely hot or cold. Visiting food scientists must wear safety equipment, including hard hats, goggles, and hearing protection.

Earnings

According to the Bureau of Labor Statistics (BLS), the median annual pay for food scientists was $63,950 in 2016. The median wage is the wage at which half the workers earned more and half earned less. The lowest-paid 10 percent of food scientists earned less than $37,660, and the highest-paid 10 percent earned more than $116,520.

Opportunities for Advancement

Recent college grads hired as food scientists usually begin their careers as assistant researchers who work on projects alongside more experienced scientists. After five years or so, food scientists can expect to move into supervisory or administrative positions, working in quality assurance, inspection, and regulation. Some senior food scientists use their experience to become corporate executives.

What Is the Future Outlook for Food Scientists?

The BLS reports that approximately 15,400 people worked as food scientists in 2014, the last year for which figures are available. Employment was projected to increase 5 percent through 2024. The fastest growth will be in areas focused on developing energy- and water-efficient food processing techniques and devising eco-friendly packaging. With a growing market for sustainable, safe, and nutritious meals, the future of food is rooted in science. Food scientists who satisfy the demand will find an abundance of employment opportunities wherever in the world food is being made.

Find Out More

American Society for Quality (ASQ)
600 N. Plankinton Ave.
Milwaukee, WI 53203
website: www.asq.org

The ASQ has over seventy-five thousand members who are focused on efficiency, effectiveness, and quality materials and resources. The society offers training, books, career information, and HACCP auditor certification.

Institute of Food Technologists (IFT)
525 W. Van Buren St.
Chicago, IL 60607
website: www.ift.org

The IFT website offers several publications, provides food scientist certifications, and hosts a Knowledge Center, which addresses numerous issues concerning food chemistry, engineering, and microbiology. The organization's Student Association offers information about competitions, scholarships, networking, and leadership opportunities.

Research Chefs Association (RCA)
330 N. Wabash Ave., Suite 2000
Chicago, IL 60611
website: www.culinology.org

The RCA is dedicated to blending the culinary arts with the science of food to provide technical information to the food industry. The association offers a certified culinary scientist accreditation and provides programs to students interested in learning food science, safety, and production techniques.

Specialty Food Association (SFA)
136 Madison Ave.
New York, NY 10016
website: www.specialtyfood.com

The Specialty Food Association is made up of culinary artists, food scientists, and food producers. The association's website features information about specialty food contests, awards, and current events. The SFA's learning center contains information about food safety, finances, trade, and sales and marketing.

Interview with a Craft Brewer

Jake Demski has been the head brewer and brewery operations manager at Greenbush Brewing Company in Sawyer, Michigan, since 2012. He answered questions about his career by e-mail.

Q: Why did you decide to become a brewer?

A: I was a fan of craft beer long before I started making it. My appreciation made me curious about the brewing industry. I had some friends in college that were really into craft beer, which piqued my interest even further. I did some home brewing myself, but only from a small-batch home brewing kit that cost under fifty dollars and made about a gallon of beer. I didn't pursue brewing that intensely until I moved back home from college and began coming to a brand-new brewery, Greenbush, which was near my home. I knew a few people who already worked there. Brewing seemed like one of those unattainable jobs until then.

Q: How did you learn to become a professional brewer?

A: I came to Greenbush with the intention of brewing beer. My brewer friends let me come in early or stay late and shadow them in my free time. I also did a lot of independent research on the Internet about beer styles and brewing and spent considerable time studying on my own. Within a few months, I was brewing beer at Greenbush.

Q: Do you think it is important for a prospective brewer to attend college?

A: I still have about twelve credits left to complete on my bachelor's degree, so I wouldn't say a college degree is necessary. That said, taking a five- or six-month master brewing course from an institution like the Siebel Institute of Technology in Chicago can almost guarantee a job at a brewery. The larger microbreweries and regional breweries make between $15 million and $20 million a year. Brewers who work there need to know how to make clean, stable, consistent beer. A solid education provides the background for a job that holds a lot of responsibility.

Q: What previous brewing-related jobs did you have before moving into your current position?

A: Everything I've learned is through personal research and on-the-job training. I started on the packaging line, washing kegs, loading bottles, and cleaning and maintaining equipment. I moved into the position of assistant brewer pretty quickly. After about two years I became head brewer, and I've been head of all brewery operations for about a year and a half now.

Q: What are some of your duties?

A: I oversee brewing, packaging, and distribution for three states. That includes production planning, material acquisition from grain to package, state and federal tax oversight, recipe and label approval, maintenance, quality control, and brewing and packaging beer.

Q: Can you describe your typical workday?

A: It changes every day, and that's part of what keeps it exciting. Some days I'll be in the brew house for twelve hours, starting around 8 a.m., when I kick off the long, complex process that transforms barley, hops, and water into beer. There's a constant ebb and flow of activity throughout the day, and I'll be transferring the brew into fermentation tanks at 7 p.m., when the Greenbush dinner rush is in full swing.

Q: What do you like most about your job?

A: The creative aspects of brewing. Since we sometimes make small batches for sale at our restaurant, I get to make unusual beers that I would never get to brew if I worked for a large microbrewery. For example, I came up with recipes for Strawberry Habanero Vanilla Ale, probably the world's weirdest combination of flavors for beer. We also brewed a small batch of Sun Spot beer especially for the solar eclipse [in August 2017].

Q: What do you like least about your job?

A: The computer work. Spreadsheets, spreadsheets, spreadsheets! I have to keep track of inventory, orders, deliveries, payments, and every drop I brew for the accountants and the government tax collectors.

Q: What personal qualities do you find most valuable for this type of work?

A: A willingness to work hard, a creative mind, a basic comprehension of math and science, and attention to detail.

Q: What advice do you have for students who might be interested in this career?

A: It's a really rewarding job, but it's not just drinking beer all day. It's a lot of hard work and long hours. The drinking beer part is just a bonus.

Other Jobs in Food and Agriculture

Agricultural economist
Agricultural equipment
    technician
Agricultural marketer
Agriculture educator
Agrophysicist
Animal breeder
Animal nutritionist
Beekeeper
Biological engineer
Botanist
Bottling line supervisor
Brewery laborer
Butcher
Candy maker
Cheese maker
Chef
Dairy buyer
Dairy processing equipment
    operator
Fish farm manager

Food broker
Food lawyer
Food product taster
Food production control
    manager
Food service manager
Food stylist
Genetic engineer
Greenhouse technician
Grocery store consultant
Horticulturist
Irrigation technician
Meatpacking plant manager
Microbiologist
Nursery manager
Nutritionist
Packaging engineer
Pest management technician
Quality control specialist
Rancher
Vineyard manager

Editor's note: The online *Occupational Outlook Handbook* of the US Department of Labor's Bureau of Labor Statistics is an excellent source of information on jobs in hundreds of career fields, including many of those listed here. The *Occupational Outlook Handbook* may be accessed online at www.bls.gov/ooh.

Index

About the Author

Stuart A. Kallen is the author of more than 350 nonfiction books for children and young adults. He has written on topics ranging from the theory of relativity to the art of electronic dance music. In addition, Kallen has written award-winning children's videos and television scripts. In his spare time he is a singer, songwriter, and guitarist in San Diego.